Cherry Jones, Richard Thompson and Joe Mantello in a scene from the Circle Repertory Company production of "The Baltimore Waltz." Set design by Loy Arcenas.

THE
BALTIMORE
WALTZ

BY **PAULA VOGEL**

★

DRAMATISTS
PLAY SERVICE
INC.

THE BALTIMORE WALTZ
Copyright ©1992, Paula Vogel

All Rights Reserved

To the memory of Carl — because I cannot sew.

Ron Vawter: ... I always saw myself as a surrogate who, in the absence of anyone else, would stand in for him. And even now, when I'm in front of an audience and I feel good, I hearken back to that feeling, that I'm standing in for them.

— *"Breaking the Rules," David Savran*

THE BALTIMORE WALTZ was produced at the Circle Repertory Company (Tanya Berezin, Artistic Director; Terrence Dwyer, Managing Director), in New York City, in February, 1992. It was directed by Anne Bogart; the set design was by Loy Arcenas; the costume design was by Walker Hicklin; the lighting design was by Dennis Parichy; the sound design and score was by John Gromada; the dramaturg was Ronn Smith and the production stage manager was Denise Yaney. The cast was as follows:

ANNA	Cherry Jones
CARL	Richard Thompson
THIRD MAN/DOCTOR	Joe Mantello

THE BALTIMORE WALTZ was produced at the Perseverance Theatre (Molly D. Smith, Artistic Director; Deborah B. Baley, Producing Director), in Douglas, Alaska, on October 18, 1990. The workshop production was directed by Annie Stokes-Hutchinson; the set design was by Bill Hudson; the costume design was by Barbara Casement and Kari Minnick; the lighting design was by John E. Miller; the sound design was by Katie Jensen and the stage manager was Carolyn Peck. The cast was as follows:

ANNA	Deborah Holbrook
CARL	Rick Bundy
THE THIRD MAN/DOCTOR	Charles Cardwell

In 1986, my brother Carl invited me to join him in a joint excursion to Europe. Due to pressures of time and money, I declined, never dreaming that he was HIV positive. This is the letter he wrote me after his first bout with pneumonia at Johns Hopkins Hospital in Baltimore, Maryland. He died on January 9, 1988.

As executor of his estate, I give permission to all future productions to reprint Carl's letter in the accompanying program. I would appreciate letting him speak to us in his own words.

The Baltimore Waltz — a journey with Carl to a Europe that exists only in the imagination — was written during the summer of 1989 at the MacDowell Colony, New Hampshire.

— Paula Vogel

March 1987

Dear Paula:

I thought I would jot down some of my thoughts about the (shall we say) production values of my ceremony. Oh God — I can hear you groaning — everybody wants to direct. Well, I want a good show, even though my role has been reduced involuntarily from player to prop.

First, concerning the choice between a religious ceremony and a memorial service. I know the family considers my Anglican observances as irrelevant as Shinto. However, I wish prayers in some recognizably traditional form to be said, prayers that give thanks to the Creator for the gift of life and the hope of reunion. For reasons which you appreciate, I prefer a woman cleric, if possible, to lead the prayers. Here are two names: Phebe Coe, Epiphany Church; the Rev. Doris Mote, Holy Evangelists. Be sure to make a generous contribution from the estate for the cleric.

As for the piece of me I leave behind, here are your options:

1) Open casket, full drag.
2) Open casket, bum up (you'll know where to place the calla lillies, won't you?).
3) Closed casket, interment with the grandparents.
4) Cremation and burial of my ashes.
5) Cremation and dispersion of my ashes in some sylvan spot.

I would really like good music. My tastes in these matters run to the highbrow: Fauré's "Pie Jesu" from his *Requiem*, Gluck's "Dance of the Blessed Spirits" from *Orfeo*, "La Vergine degli Angeli" from Verdi's *Forza*. But my favorite song is "I Dream of Jeannie," and I wouldn't mind a spiritual like "Steal Away." Also perhaps "Nearer My God to Thee." Didn't Jeannette MacDonald sing that di-vinely in *San Francisco*?

Finally, would you read or have read A.E. Housman's "Loveliest of Trees"?

Well, my dear, that's that. Should I be lain with Grandma and Papa Ben, do stop by for a visit from year to year. And feel free to chat. You'll find me a good listener.

Love,

rother

CHARACTERS

ANNA
CARL, her brother
THE THIRD MAN/DOCTOR, who also plays:
    Harry Lime
    Airport Security Guard
    Public Health Official
    Garçon
    Customs Official
    The Little Dutch Boy at Age 50
    Munich Virgin
    Radical Student Activist
    Concierge
    Dr. Todesrocheln
    and all other parts

The Baltimore Waltz takes place in a hospital (perhaps in a lounge, corridor or waiting room) in Baltimore, Maryland.

NOTES

The lighting should be highly stylized, lush, dark and imaginative, in contrast to the hospital white silence of the last scene. Wherever possible, prior to the last scene, the director is encouraged to score the production with music — every cliché of the European experience as imagined by Hollywood.

Anna might be dressed in a full slip/negligee and a trench coat. Carl is dressed in flannel pajamas and a blazer or jacket. The stuffed rabbit should be in every scene with Carl after Scene 6. The Third Man should wear latex gloves throughout the entire play.

THE BALTIMORE WALTZ

Scene 1

Three distinct areas on stage: Anna, stage right, in her trench coat, clutching the Berlitz Pocket Guide to Europe; *Carl, stage left, wearing pajamas and blazer; The Third Man/Doctor, in his lab coat and with stethoscope, is center.*

Anna reads from her book. Her accents are execrable.

ANNA. "Help me please." *(Anna recites from memory.)* Dutch: "Kunt U mij helpen, alstublieft?" "There's nothing I can do." French — *(Anna searches in vain.)* I have no memory. *(Anna reads from Berlitz.)* "Il n'y a rien à faire." "Where are the toilets?" Wo sind die Toiletten?" I've never been abroad. It's not that I don't want to — but the language terrifies me. I was traumatized by a junior high school French teacher, and after that, it was a lost cause. I think that's the reason I went into elementary education. Words like brioche, bidet, bildungsroman raise a sweat. Oh, I want to go. Carl — he's my brother, you'll meet him shortly — he desperately wants to go. But then, he can speak six languages. He's the head librarian of literature and languages at the San Francisco Public. It's a very important position. The thought of eight-hundred-year-old houses perched on the sides of mountains and rivers whose names you've only seen in the Sunday *Times* crossword puzzles — all of that is exciting. But I'm not going without him. He's read so much. I couldn't possibly go without him. You see, I've never been abroad — unless you count Baltimore, Maryland.

CARL. Good morning, boys and girls. It's Monday morning, and it's time for "Reading Hour with Uncle Carl" once again, here at the North Branch of the San Francisco Public Library. This is going to be a special reading hour. It's my very last reading hour with you. Friday will be my very last day with the San Francisco Public as children's librarian. Why? Do any of you know what a pink slip is? *(Carl holds up a rectangle of pink.)* It means I'm going on a paid leave of absence for two weeks. Shelley Bizio, the branch supervisor, has given me my very own pink slip. I got a pink slip because I wear this — *(He points to a pink triangle on his lapel.)* A pink triangle. Now, I want you all to take the pink construction paper in front of you, and take your scissors, and cut out pink triangles. There's tape at every table, so you can wear them too! Make some for Mom and Dad, and your brothers and sisters. Very good. Very good, Fabio. Oh, that's a beautiful pink triangle, Tse Heng. Now before we read our last story together, I thought we might have a sing-along. Your parents can join in, if they'd like to. Oh, don't be shy. Let's do "Here We Go Round the Mulberry Bush." Remember that one? *(He begins to sing. He also demonstrates.)* "Here we go round the mulberry bush, the mulberry bush, the mulberry bush:/ Here we go round the mulberry bush, so early in the morning." "This is the way we pick our nose, pick our nose, pick our nose:/ This is the way we pick our nose, so early in the morning." Third verse! *(He makes a rude gesture with his middle finger.)* "This is the way we go on strike, go on strike, go on strike:/ this is the way we go on strike, so early in the —" What, Mrs. Bizio? I may leave immediately? I do not have to wait until Friday to collect unemployment? Why, thank you, Mrs. Bizio. Well, boys and girls, Mrs. Bizio will take over now. Bear with her, she's personality-impaired. I want you to be very good and remember me. I'm leaving for an immediate vacation with my sister on the east coast, and I'll think of you as I travel. Remember to wear those pink triangles. *(To his supervisor.)* I'm going. I'm going. You don't have to be rude. They enjoyed it. We'll take it up with the union. *(Shouting.)* In a language you might understand, up-pay ours-yay!

ANNA.   It's the language that terrifies me.

CARL.   Lesson Number One: Subject position. I. Je. Ich. Ik. I'm sorry. Je regrette. Es tut mir leid.

ANNA.   But we decided to go when the doctor gave us his verdict.

DOCTOR. I'm sorry.

CARL. I'm sorry.

DOCTOR. There's nothing we can do.

ANNA. But what?

CARL. How long?

ANNA. Explain it to me. Very slowly. So I can understand. Excuse me, could you tell me again?

DOCTOR. There are exudative and proliferative inflammatory alterations of the endocardium, consisting of necrotic debris, fibrinoid material, and disintegrating fibroblastic cells.

CARL. Oh, sweet Jesus.

DOCTOR. It may be acute or subacute, caused by various bacteria: streptococci, staphylococci, enterococci, gonococci, gram negative bacilli, etc. It may be due to other micro-organisms, of course, but there is a high mortality rate with or without treatment. And there is usually rapid destruction and metastases.

CARL. Anna —

ANNA. I'm right here, darling. Right here.

CARL. Could you explain it very slowly?

DOCTOR. Also known as Loffler's syndrome, i.e., eosinophilia, resulting in fibroblastic thickening, persistent tachycardia, hepatomegaly, splenomegaly, serious effusions into the pleural cavity with edema. It may be Brugia malayi or Wuchereria bancofti — also known as Weingarten's syndrome. Often seen with effusions, either exudate or transudate.

ANNA. Carl —

CARL. I'm here, darling. Right here.

ANNA. It's the language that terrifies me.

Scene 2

CARL. Medical Straight Talk: Part One.

ANNA. So you're telling me that you really don't know?

DOCTOR. I'm afraid that medical science has only a small foothold in this area. But of course, it would be of great benefit to our knowledge if you would consent to observation here at Johns Hopkins —

CARL. Why? Running out of laboratory rats?!

ANNA. Oh, no. I'm sorry. I can't do that. Can you tell me at least how it was ... contracted?

DOCTOR. Well — we're not sure, yet. It's only a theory at this stage, but one that seems in great favor at the World Health Organization. We think it comes from the old cultus ornatus —

CARL. Toilet seats?

ANNA. Toilet seats! My God. Mother was right. She always said —

CARL. And never, ever, in any circumstances, in bus stations —

ANNA. Toilet seats? Cut down in the prime of youth by a toilet seat?

DOCTOR. Anna — I may call you Anna? — you teach school, I believe?

ANNA. Yes, first grade. What does that have —

DOCTOR. Ah, yes. We're beginning to see a lot of this in elementary schools. Anna — I may call you Anna? With assurances of complete confidentiality — we need to ask you very specific questions about the body, body fluids, and body functions. As mature adults, as scientists and educators. To speak frankly — when you needed to relieve yourself — where did you make wa-wa?

ANNA. There's a faculty room. But why — how — ?

DOCTOR. You never, ever used the johnny in your classroom?

ANNA. Well, maybe once or twice. There's no lock, and Robbie Matthews always tries to barge in. Sometimes I just can't get the time to — surely you're not suggesting that —

DOCTOR. You did use the facilities in your classroom? *(The Doctor makes notes from this.)*

CARL. Is that a crime? When you've got to go, you've got to —

ANNA. I can't believe that my students would transmit

something like this —

DOCTOR.   You have no idea. Five-year-olds can be deadly. It seems to be an affliction, so far, of single schoolteachers. Schoolteachers with children of their own develop an immunity to ATD ... Acquired Toilet Disease.

ANNA.   I see. Why hasn't anybody heard of this disease?

DOCTOR.   Well, first of all, the Center for Disease Control doesn't wish to inspire an all-out panic in communities. Secondly, we think education on this topic is the responsibility of the NEA, not the government. And if word of this pestilence gets out inappropriately, the PTA is going to be all over the school system demanding mandatory testing of every toilet seat in every lavatory. It's kindling for a political disaster.

ANNA.   *(Taking the Doctor aside.)* I want to ask you something confidentially. Something that my brother doesn't need to hear. What's the danger of transmission?

DOCTOR.   There's really no danger to anyone in the immediate family. You must use precautions.

ANNA.   Because what I want to know is ... can you transmit this thing by ... by doing — what exactly do you mean by precautions?

DOCTOR.   Well, I guess you should do what your mother always told you. You know, wash your hands before and after going to the bathroom. And never lick paper money or coins in any currency.

ANNA.   So there's no danger to anyone by ... what I mean, Doctor, is that I can't infect anyone by —

DOCTOR.   Just use precautions.

ANNA.   Because, in whatever time this schoolteacher has left, I intend to fuck my brains out.

DOCTOR.   Which means, in whatever time is left, she can fuck her brains out.

Scene 3

Carl and the Doctor.

CARL. *(Agitated.)* I'll tell you what. If Sandra Day O'Connor sat on just one infected potty, the media would be clamoring to do articles on ATD. If just one grandchild of George Bush caught this thing during toilet training, that would be the last we'd hear about the space program. Why isn't someone doing something?! I'm sorry. I know you're one of the converted. You're doing ... well, everything you can. I'd like to ask you something in confidence, something my sister doesn't need to hear. Is there any hope at all?

DOCTOR. Well, I suppose there's ... always hope.

CARL. Any experimental drugs? Treatments?

DOCTOR. Well, they're trying all sorts of things abroad. Our hands are tied here by NIH and the FDA, you understand. There is a long-shot avenue to explore, nothing, you understand, that I personally endorse, but there is an eighty-year-old urologist overseas who's been working in this field for some time —

CARL. We'll try anything.

DOCTOR. His name is Dr. Todesrocheln. He's somewhat unorthodox, outside the medical community in Vienna. It's gonna cost you. Mind you, this is not an endorsement.

ANNA. You hear the doctor through a long-distance corridor. Your ears are functioning, but the mind is numb. You try to listen as you swim towards his sentences in the flourescent light in his office. But you don't believe it at first. This is how I'd like to die: with dignity. No body secretions — like Merle Oberon in *Wuthering Heights*. With a somewhat becoming flush, and a transcendental gaze. Luminous eyes piercing the veil of mortal existence. The windows are open to the fresh breeze blowing off the moors. Oh. And violins in the background would be nice, too. *(Music: violins playing Strauss swell in the background.)*

14

Scene 4

The Phone Call.

THE THIRD MAN.   Lesson Number Two: Basic dialogue.
The phone call. Hello. I would like to speak to Mr. Lime,
please.
CARL.   Entschuldigen Sie, bitte — operator? Operator?
Hello? Guten Tag? Kann ich bitte mit Herr Lime sprechen?
Harry? Harry? Wie geht es dir?! Listen, I ... can you hear ...
no, I'm in Baltimore ... yeah, not since Hopkins ... no, there's
— well, there is something up. No, dear boy, that hasn't been
up in a long time — no, seriously — it's my sister. ATD.
THE THIRD MAN.   ATD? Jesus, that's tough, old man.
You've got to watch where you sit these days. She's a sweet
kid. Yeah. Yeah. Wait a second. *(Offstage.)* Inge? Inge, baby?
Ein Bier, bitte, baby. Ja. Ja. You too, baby. *(Pause.)* Okay. Dr.
Todesrocheln? Yeah, you might say I know him. But don't
tell anybody I said that. There's also a new drug they've got
over here. Black market. I might be able to help you. I said
might. But it's gonna cost you. *(Cautiously, ominously.)* Do you
still have the rabbit?
CARL.   I'll bring the rabbit.
THE THIRD MAN.   Good. A friend of mine will be in
touch. And listen, old man ... if anybody asks you, you don't
know me. I'll see you in a month. You know where to find
me.
THE THIRD MAN and CARL.   *(Simultaneously.)* Click.

Scene 5

THE THIRD MAN.   Lesson Number Three: Pronouns and the possessive case. I, you, he, she and it. Me, you, their. Yours, mine, and ours.

VOICE OF ANNA.   There's nothing I can do. There's nothing you can do. There's nothing he, she or it can do. There's nothing we can do. There's nothing they can do.

ANNA.   So what are we going to do?

CARL.   Start packing, sister dear.

ANNA.   Europe? You mean it?

CARL.   We'll mosey about France and Germany, and then work our way down to Vienna.

ANNA.   What about your job?

CARL.   It's only a job.

ANNA.   It's a very important job! Head of the entire San Francisco Public —

CARL.   They'll hold my job for me. I'm due for a leave.

ANNA.   Oh, honey. Can we afford this?

CARL.   It's only money.

ANNA.   It's your money.

CARL.   It's our money.

Scene 6

THE THIRD MAN.   Lesson Four: Present tense of faire. What are we going to do? Qu'est-ce qu'on va faire.

ANNA.   So what are we going to do?

CARL.   We'll see this doctor in Vienna.

ANNA.   Dr. Todesrocheln?

CARL.   We have to try.

ANNA.   A urologist?

CARL.   He's working on a new drug.

ANNA.   A European urologist?

CARL.   What options do we have?

ANNA.   Wait a minute. What are his credentials? Who is this

16

guy?

CARL. He was trained at the Allgemeines Krankenhaus during the Empire.

ANNA. Yeah? Just what was he doing from, say, 1938 to 1945? Research?

CARL. It's best not to ask too many questions. There are people who swear by his work.

ANNA. What's his specialty?

CARL. Well, actually, he's a practitioner of uriposia.

ANNA. He writes poems about urine?

CARL. No. He drinks it.

ANNA. I'm not going.

CARL. Let's put off judgement until we arrange a consultation ... my god, you're so messy. Look at how neat my suitcase is in comparison. You'll never find a thing in there.

ANNA. I refuse to drink my own piss for medical science. *(Carl grabs a stuffed rabbit and thrusts it in Anna's suitcase.)* What are you doing?

CARL. We can't leave bunny behind.

ANNA. What is a grown man like you doing with a stuffed rabbit?

CARL. I can't sleep without bunny.

ANNA. I didn't know you slept with ... stuffed animals.

CARL. There's a lot you don't know about me.

Scene 7

THE THIRD MAN. Lesson Five: Basic dialogue. At the airport. We are going to Paris. What time does our flight leave? Nous allons à Paris. A quelle heure depart notre vol? *(The Third Man becomes an Airport Security Guard.)*

AIRPORT SECURITY GUARD. Okay. Next. Please remove your keys and all other metallic items. Place all belongings on the belt. Next. *(Carl and Anna carry heavy luggage. Carl halts.)*

CARL. Wait. I need your suitcase. *(He opens Anna's luggage and begins to rummage around.)*

ANNA. Hey!

CARL. It was a mess to begin with. Ah — *(He retrieves the stuffed rabbit.)* There.

ANNA. Are you having an anxiety attack?

CARL. You hold it. *(He and Anna stamp, sit and stand on the baggage. Carl manages to relock the bag.)*

ANNA. What is wrong with you?

CARL. X-rays are bad for bunny.

AIRPORT SECURITY GUARD. Next. Please remove all metallic objects. Keys. Eyeglasses. Gold Fillings.

CARL. Go on. You first.

AIRPORT SECURITY GUARD. Metallic objects? *(Anna passes through, holding the stuffed rabbit. Carl sighs, relieved. Carl passes through. The Airport Security Guard stops him.)* One moment, please. *(The Airport Security Guard almost strip searches him. He uses a metallic wand which makes loud, clicking noises. Finally, he nods. He hands Anna and Carl their bags, still suspiciously looking at Carl.)*

ANNA. Okay, bunny — Paris, here we come!

Scene 8

THE THIRD MAN. At the hotel. *(Simultaneously with Carl's next lines.)* Lesson Six. Direct pronouns. I am tired. And my sister looks at herself in the mirror.

CARL. Sixieme Leçon: Pronoms — compléments directs. Je suis fatigué. Et ma soeur — elle se regarde dans la glace. *(Carl climbs into a double bed with the stuffed rabbit. Anna stares into a mirror. The Third man, apart, stands in their bedroom.)*

THE THIRD MAN. The first separation — your first sense of loss. You were five — your brother was seven. Your parents would not let you sleep in the same bed anymore. They removed you to your own bedroom. You were too old, they said. But every now and then, when they turned off the lights and went downstairs — when the dark scared you, you would rise and go to him. And he would let you nestle under his arm, under the covers, where you would fall to sleep, breathing in the scent of your own breath and his seven-year-old body.

CARL.   Come to bed, sweetie. Bunny and I are waiting. We're going to be jet-lagged for a while.

ANNA.   *(Anna continues to stare in the mirror.)* It doesn't show yet.

CARL.   No one can tell. Let's get some sleep, honey.

ANNA.   I don't want anyone to know.

CARL.   It's not a crime. It's an illness.

ANNA.   I don't want anybody to know.

CARL.   It's your decision. Just don't tell anyone ... what ... you do for a living. *(Anna joins Carl in the bed. He holds her hand.)*

ANNA.   Well, there's one good thing about traveling in Europe ... and about dying.

CARL.   What's that?

ANNA.   I get to sleep with you again.

Scene 9

CARL.   Medical Straight Talk: Part Two. *(The Third Man becomes a Public Health Official.)*

PUBLIC HEALTH OFFICIAL.   Here at the Department of Health and Human Services we are announcing Operation Squat. There is no known cure for ATD right now, and we are acknowledging the urgency of this dread disease by recognizing it as our 82nd national health priority. Right now ATD is the fourth major cause of death of single schoolteachers, ages 24 to 40 ... behind school buses, lockjaw and playground accidents. The best policy, until a cure can be found, is of education and prevention. *(Anna and Carl hold up posters of a toilet seat in a circle with a red diagonal slash.)* If you are in the high risk category — single elementary school teachers, classroom aides, custodians and playground drug pushers — follow these simple guides. *(Anna and Carl hold up copies of the educational pamphlets.)*

Do: Use the facilities in your own home before departing for school.

Do: Use the facilities in your own home as soon as you return from school.

Do: Hold it.

Don't: Eat meals in public restrooms.

Don't: Flush lavatory equipment and then suck your digits.

If absolutely necessary to relieve yourself at work, please remember the Department of Health and Human Services ATD slogan: Do squat, don't sit.

Scene 10

Music: accordion playing a song like "La Vie en Rose."*
Anna and Carl stroll.

CARL.   Of course, the Left Bank has always been a haven for outcasts, foreigners and students, since the time that Abélard fled the Ile de La Cité to found the university here —

ANNA.   Oh, look. Is that the Eiffel Tower? It looks so ... phallic.

CARL.   And it continued to serve as a haven for the avantgarde of the Twenties, the American expatriate community that could no longer afford Montparnesse —

ANNA.   My god, they really do smoke Gauloise here.

CARL.   And, of course, the Dada and Surrealists who set up camp here after World War I and their return from Switzerland — *(The Third Man, in a trench coat and red beret, crosses the stage.)*

ANNA.   Are we being followed?

CARL.   Is your medication making you paranoid? *(Pause.)* Now, over here is the famous spot where Gertrude supposedly said to her brother Leo — *(The Third Man follows them.)*

* See Special Note on copyright page.

20

ANNA. I know. "God is the answer. What is the question?" — I'm not imagining it. That man has been trailing us from the Boulevard St. Michel.

CARL. Are you getting hungry?

ANNA. I'm getting tired.

CARL. Wait. Let's just whip around the corner to the Cafe St. Michel where Hemingway, after an all-night bout, threw up his shrimp heads all over Scott's new suede shoes — which really was a moveable feast. *(The Third Man is holding an identical stuffed rabbit and looks at them.)*

ANNA. Carl! Carl! Look! That man over there!

CARL. So? They have stuffed rabbits over here, too. Let's go.

ANNA. Why is he following us? He's got the same —

CARL. It's your imagination. How about a little déjeuner? *(Anna and Carl walk to a small table and chairs.)*

Scene 11

GARÇON. *(With a thick Peter Sellers French.)* It was a simple bistro affair by French standards. He had le veau Prince Orloff, she le boeuf à la mode — a simple dish of haricots verts, and a médoc to accompany it all. He barely touched his meal. She mopped the sauces with the bread. As their meal progressed, Anna thought of the lunches she packed back home. For the past ten years, hunched over in the faculty room at McCormick Elementary, this is what Anna ate: on Mondays, pressed chipped chicken sandwiches with mayonnaise on white; on Tuesdays, soggy tuna sandwiches; on Wednesdays, Velveeta cheese and baloney; on Thursdays, drier pressed chicken on the now stale white bread; on Fridays, Velveeta and tuna. She always had a small wax envelope of carrot sticks or celery, and a can of Diet Pepsi. Anna, as she ate in the bistro, wept. What could she know of love?

CARL. Why are you weeping?

ANNA. It's just so wonderful.

CARL. You're a goose.

ANNA. I've wasted over thirty years on convenience foods. *(The Garçon approaches the table.)*

GARÇON. Is everything all right?

ANNA. Oh god. Yes — yes — it's wonderful.

CARL. My sister would like to see the dessert tray. *(Anna breaks out in tears again. The Garçon shrugs and exits. He reappears two seconds later as The Third Man, this time with a trench coat and blue beret. He sits at an adjacent table and stares in their direction.)*

ANNA. Who is that man? Do you know him?

CARL. *(Carl hastily looks at The Third Man.)* No, I've never seen him before. *(The Third Man brings the stuffed rabbit out of his trench coat.)*

ANNA. He's flashing his rabbit at you.

CARL. *(Carl rises.)* Excuse me. I think I'll go to les toilettes.

ANNA. Carl! Be careful! Don't sit! *(Carl exits. The Third Man waits a few seconds, looks at Anna, and then follows Carl without expression.)* What is it they do with those rabbits? *(A split second later, the Garçon reenters with the dessert tray. Anna ogles him.)*

GARÇON. O-kay. We have la crème plombière pralinée, un bavarois à l'orange, et ici we have une Charlotte Malakoff aux Framboises. Our specialité is le gâteau de crêpes à la Normande. What would mademoiselle like? *(Anna has obviously not been looking at the dessert tray.)*

ANNA. *(Sighing.)* Ah, yes.

GARÇON. *(The Garçon smiles.)* Vous êtes Américaîne? This is your first trip to Paris?

ANNA. Yes.

GARÇON. And you do not speak at all French?

ANNA. No. *(The Garçon smiles.)*

GARÇON. *(Suggestively.)* Bon. Would you like la specialité de la maison?

Scene 12

CARL. Exercise: La Carte. La specialité de la maison. Back at the hotel, Anna sampled the Garçon's specialité de la maison while her brother browsed the Louvre. *(Anna and the Garçon are shapes beneath the covers of the bed. Carl clutches his stuffed rabbit.)* Jean Baptiste Camille Corot lived from 1796 to 1875. Although he began his career by studying in the classical tradition, his later paintings reveal the influence of the Italian style.

ANNA. *(Muffled.)* Ah! Yes!

GARÇON. *(Also muffled.)* Ah! Oui!

CARL. He traveled extensively around the world, and in the salon of 1827 his privately lauded techniques were displayed in public.

ANNA. Yes — oh, yes, yes!

GARÇON. Mais oui!

CARL. Before the Academy had accepted realism, Corot's progressive paintings, his clear sighted observations of nature, revealed a fresh almost spritely quality of light, tone and composition.

ANNA. Yes — that's right — faster —

GARÇON. Plus vite?

ANNA. Faster —

GARÇON. Encore! Plus vite!

ANNA. Wait!

GARÇON. Attends?

CARL. It was his simplicity, and his awareness of color that brought a fresh wind into the staid academy —

GARÇON. Maintenant?

ANNA. Lower — faster — lower —

GARCON. Plus bas — plus vite — plus bas —

CARL. He was particularly remembered and beloved for his championing the cause of younger artists with more experimental techniques, bringing the generosity of his advancing reputation to their careers.

ANNA. Yes – I – I — I — I — !

GARÇON. Je — je! Je!! Je! *(Pause.)*
CARL. In art, as in life, some things need no translation.
GARÇON. Gauloise?
CARL. For those of you who are interested, in the next room are some stunning works by Delacroix.

Scene 13

Back at the Hotel.

CARL. Lesson Seven: Basic vocabulary. Parts of the body. *(Carl, slightly out of the next scene, watches them. Anna sits up in bed. The Garçon is asleep beneath the sheet.)*
ANNA. I did read one book once in French. *Le Petit Prince.* Lying here, watching him sleep, I look at his breast and remember the Rose with its single, pathetic thorn for protection. And here — his puckered red nipple, lying poor and vulnerable on top of his blustering breast plate. It's really so sweet about men. *(She kisses the Garçon's breast. The Garçon stirs.)*
GARÇON. Encore?
ANNA. What is the word — in French — for this? *(She fingers his breast.)*
GARÇON. For un homme — le sein. For une femme — la mamelle.
ANNA. Le sein?
GARÇON. Oui. Le sein.
ANNA. *(She kisses his neck.)* And this?
GARÇON. Le Cou.
ANNA. Et ici?
GARÇON. Bon. Décolleté — *(Anna begins to touch him under the sheet.)*
ANNA. And this?
GARÇON. *(The Garçon laughs.)* S'il vous plâit ... I am tickling there. Ah. Couille.
ANNA. Culle?
GARÇON. Non. Couille. Le cul is something much different. Ici c'est le cul.

ANNA.   Oh, yes. That's very different.

GARÇON.   *(Taking her hand under the sheet.)* We sometimes call these also Le Quatrième État. The Fourth Estate.

ANNA.   Really? Because they enjoy being "scooped"?

GARÇON.   Bien sûr.

ANNA.   And this?

GARÇON.   *(With pride.)* Ah. Ma Tour Eiffel. I call it aussi my Charles DeGalle.

ANNA.   Wow.

GARÇON.   My grandfather called his Napoleon.

ANNA.   I see. I guess it runs in your family.

GARÇON.   *(Modestly.)* Oui. Grand-mère — qu'est-ce que c'est le mot en anglais? Her con — here — ici — do you know what I am meaning?

ANNA.   You're making yourself completely clear —

GARÇON.   We called hers the Waterloo de mon grand-père — *(Anna digs under the sheet more.)*

ANNA.   And this?

GARÇON.   *(The Garçon is scandalized.)* Non. There is no word en français. Pas du tout.

ANNA.   For this? There must be —

GARÇON.   Non! Only the Germans have a word for that. *(Carl enters and casually converses with Anna. Startled, the Garçon covers himself with the sheet.)*

CARL.   Hello, darling. Are you feeling better? *(Carl walks to the chair beside the bed and removes the Garçon's clothing.)*

ANNA.   Yes, much. I needed to lie down. How was the Louvre? *(The Garçon carefully rises from the bed and takes his clothing from Carl, who is holding them out. He creeps cautiously stage left and begins to pull on his clothes.)*

CARL.   Oh, Anna. I'm so sorry you missed it. The paintings of David were amazing. The way his paintbrush embraced the body — it was just incredible to stand there and see them in the flesh.

ANNA.   Ah yes — in the flesh. *(She smiles at the confused Garçon.)*

CARL.   Well, sweetie. It's been a thoroughly rewarding day for both of us. I'm for turning in. How about you? *(The*

25

Garçon is now fully dressed.)
ANNA.   Yes, I'm tired. Here — I've warmed the bed for you.
(She throws back the sheet.)
CARL.   Garçon — l'addition!
ANNA.   *(To the Garçon.)* Merci beaucoup. *(Anna blows him a
kiss. The Garçon takes a few steps out of the scene as Carl climbs
into bed.)*

Scene 14

THE THIRD MAN.   Anna has a difficult time sleeping. She
is afflicted with night thoughts. According to Elizabeth Kübler-
Ross, there are six stages the terminal patient travels in the
course of her illness. The first stage: Denial and Isolation.
*(The Third Man stays in the hotel room and watches Carl and Anna
in the bed. They are sleeping, when Anna sits upright.)*
ANNA.   I feel so alone. The ceiling is pressing down on me.
I can't believe I am dying. Only at night. Only at night. In
the morning, when I open my eyes, I feel absolutely well —
without a body. And then the thought comes crashing in my
mind. This is the last spring I may see. This is the last summer. It can't be. There must be a mistake. They mixed the
specimens up in the hospital. Some poor person is walking
around, dying, with the false confidence of my prognosis,
thinking themselves well. It's a clerical error. Carl! I can't
sleep. Do you think they made a mistake?
CARL.   Come back to sleep —   *(Carl pulls Anna down on the
bed to him, and strokes her brow. They change positions on the bed.)*
THE THIRD MAN.   The second stage: Anger.
ANNA.   *(Anna sits bolt upright in bed, angry.)* How could this
happen to me! I did my lesson plans faithfully for the past
ten years! I've taught in classrooms without walls — kept up
on new audio-visual aids — I read Summerhill! And I believed
it! When the principal assigned me the job of the talent show
— and nobody wants to do the talent show — I pleaded for
cafeteria duty, bus duty — but no, I got stuck with the talent
show. And those kids put on the best darn show that school

has ever seen! Which one of them did this to me? Emily Baker? For slugging Johnnie MacIntosh? Johnnie MacIntosh? Because I sent him home for exposing himself to Susy Higgins? Susy Higgins? Because I called her out on her nosepicking? Or those Nader twins? I've spent the best years of my life giving to those kids — it's not —

CARL. Calm down, sweetie. You're angry. It's only natural to be angry. Elizabeth Kübler-Ross says that —

ANNA. What does she know about what it feels like to die?! Elizabeth Kübler-Ross can sit on my face! *(Carl and Anna change positions on the bed.)*

THE THIRD MAN. The third stage: Bargaining.

ANNA. Do you think if I let Elizabeth Kübler-Ross sit on my face I'll get well? *(Carl and Anna change positions on the bed.)*

THE THIRD MAN. The fourth stage: Depression. *(Carl sits on the side of the bed beside Anna.)*

CARL. Anna — honey — come on, wake up.

ANNA. Leave me alone.

CARL. Come on, sweetie ... you've been sleeping all day now, and you slept all yesterday. Do you want to sleep away our last day in France?

ANNA. Why bother?

CARL. You've got to eat something. You've got to fight this. For me.

ANNA. Leave me alone. *(Carl lies down beside Anna. They change positions.)*

THE THIRD MAN. The fifth stage: Acceptance. *(Anna and Carl are lying in bed, awake. They hold hands.)*

ANNA. When I'm gone, I want you to find someone.

CARL. Let's not talk about me.

ANNA. No, I want to. It's important to me to know that you'll be happy and taken care of after ... when I'm gone.

CARL. Please.

ANNA. I've got to talk about it. We've shared everything else. I want you to know how it feels ... what I'm thinking ... when I hold your hand, and I kiss it ... I try to memorize what it looks like, your hand ... I wonder if there's any memory in the grave?

THE THIRD MAN. And then there's the sixth stage: Hope. *(Anna and Carl rise from the bed.)*
CARL. How are you feeling?
ANNA. I feel good today.
CARL. Do you feel like traveling?
ANNA. Yes. It would be nice to see Amsterdam. Together. We might as well see as much as we can while I'm well —
CARL. That's right, sweetie. And maybe you can eat something —
ANNA. I'm hungry. That's a good sign, don't you think?
CARL. That's a wonderful sign. You'll see. You'll feel better when you eat.
ANNA. Maybe the doctor in Vienna can help.
CARL. That's right.
ANNA. What's drinking a little piss? It can't hurt you.
CARL. Right. Who knows? We've got to try.
ANNA. I'll think of it as ... European lager.
CARL. Golden Heidelberg. *(Carl and Anna hum/sing a song such as the drinking song from* The Student Prince.*)*

Scene 15

THE THIRD MAN. And as Anna and Carl took the train into Holland, the seductive swaying of the TEE-train aroused another sensation. Unbeknownst to Elizabeth Kübler-Ross, there is a seventh stage for the dying. There is a growing urge to fight the sickness of the body with the health of the body. The seventh stage: Lust. *(Anna and Carl are seated in a train compartment. Carl holds the stuffed rabbit out to Anna.)*
ANNA. Why?
CARL. Just take it. Hold it for me. Just through customs.

* See Special Note on copyright page.

28

ANNA.   Only if you tell me why.

CARL.   Don't play games right now. Or we'll be in deep, deep do-do. *(Anna reluctantly takes the stuffed rabbit and holds it.)*

ANNA.   You're scaring me.

CARL.   I'm sorry, sweetie. You're the only one I can trust to hold my rabbit. Trust me. It's important.

ANNA.   Then why won't you tell me — ?

CARL.   There are some some things you're better off not knowing.

ANNA.   Are you smuggling drugs? Jewels?

CARL.   *(Whispers.)* It's beyond measure. It's invaluable to me. That's all I'll say. *(In a louder tone.)* Just act normal now.

CUSTOMS OFFICIAL.   Uw paspoort, alstublieft. *(Anna and Carl give him their passports. Carl is nervous. Anna smiles at the Customs Official a bit laciviously.)* Have you anything to declare?

ANNA.   *(Whispering.)* Yes — captain, I'm smuggling contraband. I demand to be searched. In private.

CUSTOMS OFFICIAL.   *(The Customs Official blushes.)* Excuse me?

ANNA.   Yes. I said — waar is het damestoilet?

CUSTOMS OFFICIAL.   Oh ... I thought ... *(The Customs Official giggles.)*

ANNA.   Yes?

CUSTOMS OFFICIAL.   First left. *(The Customs Official returns their passports.)* Have a very pleasant stay. *(Anna waves bunny's arm goodbye. The Customs Official looks at her, blushes again, and retreats. Carl relaxes.)*

CARL.   You're good at this. Very good.

ANNA.   When in Holland, do like the Dutch ... Mata Hari was Dutch, you know.

Scene 16

CARL.   Questions sur le Dialogue. Est-ce que les hommes Hollandais sont comme les Français? Are Dutch men like the French? *(Anna and The Little Dutch Boy at Age 50. He wears traditional wooden shoes, trousers and vest. His Buster Brown haircut*

29

and hat make him look dissipated.)

THE LITTLE DUTCH BOY AT AGE 50.   It was kermis-time, the festival in my village. And I had too much bier with my school friends, Piet and Jan. Ja. Soo — Piet thought we should go to the outer dyke with cans of spray paint, after the kermis. So we went.

Here in Noord Brabant there are three walls of defenses against the cruelty of the North Sea. The first dyke is called the Waker — the Watcher; the second dyke is de Slaper — the Sleeper; and the last dyke, which had never before been tested, is known as the Dromer — the Dreamer.

And when we got to the Dreamer, Piet said to me: "Willem, you do it." Meaning I was to write on the walls of the Dreamer. This is why I was always in trouble in school — Piet and Jan would say, "Willem, you do it," and whatever it was — I would do it.

Soo — I took up a can of the paint and in very big letters, I wrote in Dutch that our schoolmaster, Mijnheer Van Doorn, was a gas-passer. Everyone could read the letters from far away. And just as I was finishing this, and Piet and Jan were laughing behind me, I looked — I was on my knees, pressed up against the dyke — and I could see that the wall of the Dreamer was cracking its surface, very fine little lines, like a goose egg when it breaks from within.

And I yelled to my friends — Look! And they came a bit closer, and as we looked, right above my head, a little hole began to peck its way through the clay. And there was just a small trickle of water. And Jan said: "Willem, put your thumb in that hole." And by that time, the hole in the dyke was just big enough to put my thumb in. "Why?" I asked of Jan. "Just do it," he said. And so I did.

And once I put my thumb in, I could not get it out. Suddenly we could hear the waves crashing as The Sleeper began to collapse. Only the Dreamer remained to hold off the savage water. "Help me!" I yelled to Jan and Piet — but they ran away. "Vlug!" I cried — but no one could hear me. And I stayed there, crouching, with my thumb stuck into the clay. And I thought what if the Dreamer should give in, too. How the waves would bear my body like a messenger to the village. How no one would survive the flood. Only the church steeple would remain to mark the spot where we had lived. How young we were to die. *(Pause.)*

Have you ever imagined what it would be like to be face to face with death?

ANNA.   Yes — yes I have.

THE LITTLE DUTCH BOY AT AGE 50.   And have you ever prayed for deliverance against all hope?

ANNA.   I — no. I haven't been able to get to that stage. Yet.

THE LITTLE DUTCH BOY AT AGE 50.   But the Dreamer held. And finally there came wagons with men from the village, holding lanterns and sand and straw. And they found me there, strung up by my thumb, beside the big black letters: Mijnheer Van Doorn is een gas-passer. And they freed me and said I was a hero, and I became the boy who held back the sea with his thumb.

ANNA.   Golly. You were very brave.

THE LITTLE DUTCH BOY AT AGE 50.   I was stupid. Wrong place, wrong time.

ANNA.   How long ago did this happen?

THE LITTLE DUTCH BOY AT AGE 50.   *(Sadly.)* Let us just say it happened a long time ago.

ANNA.   You've faced death. I wish my brother were here to meet you.

THE LITTLE DUTCH BOY AT AGE 50.   Where is he? Wo ist dein bruder?

ANNA.   Oh, he stayed in Amsterdam to see the Rijksmuseum and the Van Gogh Museum.

THE LITTLE DUTCH BOY AT AGE 50.   And you did not go? You should see them, they are really fantastic.

ANNA.   Why? What's the use? I won't remember them, I'll have no memory.

THE LITTLE DUTCH BOY AT AGE 50.   So you are an American?

ANNA.   Yes.

THE LITTLE DUTCH BOY AT AGE 50.   So do you want to

sleep with me? All the women toeristen want to sleep with the little Dutch boy who put his thumb in the dyke.

ANNA.   Do you mind so much?

THE LITTLE DUTCH BOY AT AGE 50.   *(Shrugs.)* Nee. It's a way to make a living, is it niet?

ANNA.   *(Quietly.)* Let's go then.

Scene 17

CARL.   Répétez. En Français. Where is my brother going? Où va mon frère? Bien.

ANNA.   I had just returned from my day trip and left the Centraal Station. The sun sparkled on the waters of the canal, and I decided to walk back to the hotel. Just then I saw my brother. *(Carl enters in a trench coat, sunglasses, holding the stuffed rabbit.)* I tried to catch up with Carl, dodging bicycles and pedestrians. And then, crossing the Amstel on the Magere Brug, he appeared. *(The Third Man enters, in a trench coat, sunglasses, and with black gloves, holding a stuffed rabbit.)* I trailed them from a discrete distance. *(The Third Man and Carl walk rapidly, not glancing at each other. Carl stops; The Third Man stops a few paces behind. Carl walks; The Third Man walks. Carl stops; The Third Man stops. Finally, they face each other and meet. Quickly, looking surreptitiously around, Carl and The Third Man stroke each other's stuffed rabbits. They quickly part and walk off in opposite directions, but not before the Third Man attempts to grab Carl's rabbit and run. Anna rushes to C., looking in both directions.)* I tried to follow the man in the trench coat, and crossed behind him over the Amstel, but I lost sight of him in the crowd of men wearing trench coats and sunglasses. I want some answers from my brother. Whatever trouble he's in, he has to share it with me. I want some answers back at the hotel. He's going to talk.

Scene 18

CARL.   Questions sur le dialogue. You must learn. Sie müssen lernen. *(Anna enters the empty hotel room. On the bed, propped up on pillows, lies a stuffed rabbit.)*
ANNA.   Carl? Carl? Are you back? Carl? *(Anna stops and looks at the stuffed rabbit.)*
CARL.   *(From the side.)* You were not permitted to play with dolls; dolls are for girls. You played with your sister's dolls until your parents found out. They gave you a stuffed animal — a thin line was drawn. Rabbits were an acceptable surrogate for little boys. You named him Jo-Jo. You could not sleep without him. Jo-Jo traveled with you to the seashore, to the hotel in New York City when you were seven, to your first summer camp. He did not have the flaxen plastic hair of your sister's Betsey-Wetsy, but he had long, furry ears, soft white on one side, pink satin inside. He let you stroke them. He never betrayed you. He taught you to trust in contact. You will love him always.
ANNA.   *(Anna moves towards the stuffed rabbit.)* My brother left you behind, did he? Alone at last. Okay, bunny, now you're going to talk. I want some answers. What have you got that's so important? *(Just as Anna reaches for the stuffed rabbit, The Third Man — in trench coat, sunglasses and black gloves — steps out into the room.)*
THE THIRD MAN.   *(Threateningly.)* I wouldn't do that, if I were you. *(Anna screams in surprise.)* Now listen. Where is your brother? I have a message for him. Tell him he's running out of time. Do you understand? *(Anna, scared, nods.)* Good. He'd better not try to dupe us. We're willing to arrange a swap — his sister for the rabbit. Tell him we're waiting for him in Vienna. And tell him he'd better bring the rabbit to the other side. *(The Third Man disappears. Anna, shaken, sits on the bed and holds the stuffed rabbit. She strokes it for comfort. Carl enters, in a frenzy. He carries his stuffed rabbit. Anna stares as Carl tosses the decoy rabbit away.)*

CARL. Don't ask me any questions. I can't tell you what's happening. Are you able to travel? Good. We have to leave Amsterdam tonight. There's a train in an hour. We'll go to Germany. Are you packed?

Scene 19

ANNA and THE THIRD MAN. *(Simultaneously.)* Wann fahrt der nächste Zug nach Hamburg? *(German band music swells as Anna and Carl sit in their railroad compartment, side by side. Anna, pale, holds the stuffed rabbit in her lap.)*

CARL. Ah, Saxony, Bavaria, the Black Forest, the Rhineland ... I love them all. I think perhaps now would be a good time to show the slides.

ANNA. I'm so sorry. I hate it when people do this to me.

CARL. Nonsense. People like to see slides of other people's trips. These are in no particular order. We'll only show a few, just to give a taste of the German countryside.

ANNA. Carl took over two hour's worth of slides.

CARL. If you'll just dim the lights, please. *(The Third Man wheels in the projector and operates it throughout the travelogue.)* Well. Bonn's as good a place to start as anywhere. This is the view from the snug little hotel we stayed in. The gateway to the Rhine, the birthplace of Beethoven, and the resting place of Schumann. *(Slide: the view of downtown Baltimore from the Ramada Inn near Johns Hopkins Hospital, overlooking the industrial harbor.)*

ANNA. Looks a lot like Baltimore to me.

CARL. My sister jests. As you can see in the slide, one night we splurged and stayed in a rather dear inn near the Drachenfels mountains, where Lord Byron had sported. *(Slide: a close-up of the balcony railing looking into the Ramada Inn hotel room.)*

ANNA. *(Dead-panned.)* This is the room I slept in while I stayed with my brother Carl. *(Slide: gutted ruins of inner-city Baltimore near the Jones-Fall Expressway; rubble and obvious urban blight.)*

CARL. Alas, poor Köln. Practically wiped out by airplane raids during World War II, and yet, out of this destruction, the cathedral of Köln managed to survive — one of the most beautiful Gothic churches in the world, with a superb altar painted by the master artist of Köln, Stefan Lochner. *(Slide: an impoverished storefront church, a black evangelical sect in Baltimore.)* Let's see — what do we have next? *(Slide: a Sabrett's hotdog cart with its blue and orange umbrella in front of Johns Hopkins Hospital.)* Oh, yes. Let's talk about the food. Whereas I snapped momentos of the regal pines of the Black Forest, Anna insisted on taking photos of everything she ate.

ANNA. I can remember things I feel.

CARL. Well, then, let's talk about the food. Germany has a more robust gustatory outlook than the delicate palate of France. The Germans positively celebrate the pig from snout to tail. I could not convince Anna to sample the Sulperknochen, which is a Rheingau concoction of ears, snout, tail and feet.

ANNA. Ugh. *(Slide: a close-up of vender placing a hot-dog on a bun and lathering it with mustard; there are canned sodas in a wide variety.)*

CARL. And of course, everything is washed down with beer. *(Slide: Anna sipping a Bud Lite.)*

ANNA. It was delicious.

CARL. Enough of food. May we talk about culture, sister, dear? Next slide, please. *(Slide: the Maryland National Armory, the state penitentiary.)* Ah, Heidelberg. Dueling scars and castles. Spectacular ruin which serves as the locale for open-air concerts and fireworks ... *(Slide: the Baltimore smokestack.)* ... and by a quaint cable car, you can reach the peak at Königstuhl, 2,000 feet high, with its breathtaking view of the Neckar Valley. *(Slide: the Bromo Seltzer tower in Baltimore. Slide: the interstate highways viewed from the tower.)* Every cobblestoned street, every alleyway, was so pristine and clean. *(Slide: the row-houses on Monument Street. Slide: a corridor of Johns Hopkins Hospital, outside the basement laboratories.)* Wasn't it, Anna?

ANNA. *(Dead-pan.)* Yes. Sterile. *(Slide: a hospital aide washing the floor.)*

CARL.   Even the Black Forest looked swept. We splurged once again and stayed at the Waldhorn Post here, outside of Wildbad. *(Slide: exterior of Johns Hopkins Hospital.)* The hotel dates back to 1145 — the chef there is renown for his game dishes. *(Slide: Anna in front of a vending machine dispensing wrapped sandwiches in the Johns Hopkins Hospital cafeteria.)*

ANNA.   I wasn't too hungry.

CARL.   I was ravenous. *(Slides: Route 95 outside the harbor tunnel; the large toll signs are visible.)* Let's see — the Romantic Road ... die Romantishe Strasse ... a trek through picture-book Bavaria and the Allgau Alpen ... Füssen to Wurzburg.

ANNA.   Honey, perhaps they've seen enough. It's hard to sit through this many —

CARL.   Wait. Just one more. They've got to see Neuschwanstein, built by mad King Ludwig II. It's so rococo it's Las Vegas. *(Slide: the castle at Disneyland.)* I believe that Ludwig was reincarnated in the twentieth century as Liberace. Wait a moment, that's not the castle.

ANNA.   Yes, it is.

CARL.   *(Upset.)* It looks like — how did that get in here?

ANNA.   I don't know which castle you're referring to, but it's definitely a castle. *(Slide: a close-up of the castle, with a large Mickey Mouse in the picture.)*

CARL.   That's not funny, Anna! Are you making fun of me?

ANNA.   Don't get upset. *(Slide: Donald Duck has joined Mickey Mouse with tourists.)*

CARL.   I went to Europe. I walked through Bavaria and the Black Forest. I combed through Neuschwanstein! I did these things, and I will remember the beauty of it all my life! I don't appreciate your mockery !

ANNA.   It's just a little —

CARL.   You went through Germany on your back. All you'll remember are hotel ceilings. You can show them your Germany — *(He rushes off, angry.)*

ANNA.   Sometimes my brother gets upset for no apparent reason. Some wires cross in his brain and he — I'm sorry. Lights, please. *(The Third Man wheels the projector off-stage.)* I would like to show you my impressions of Germany. They were something like this —

Scene 20

In Munich. Anna is under the sheet beside the Munich Virgin, who is very young.

ANNA.   Are you comfortable?

MUNICH VIRGIN.   Ja, ja ... danke.

ANNA.   Good. Have you been the bellhop here for a long time?

MUNICH VIRGIN.   Not so very long a time. My vater owns the hotel, and says I must learn and work very hard. Soon I will be given the responsibility of the front desk.

ANNA.   My. That's exciting. *(Pause.)* Are you cold?

MUNICH VIRGIN.   Nein. Just a ... klein nervös. My English is not so very good.

ANNA.   Is this your first time? You always remember your first time. *(Pause.)* I'm very honored. *(Pause.)* Listen. I'm a schoolteacher. May I tell you something? A little lesson? When you're a much older man, and you've loved many women, you'll be a wonderful lover if you're just a little bit nervous ... like you are right now. Because it will always be the first time.

MUNICH VIRGIN.   You are a very nice woman.

ANNA.   The human body is a wonderful thing. Like yours. Like mine. The beauty of the body heals all the sickness, all the bad things that happen to it. And I really want you to feel this. Because if you feel it, you'll remember it. And then maybe you'll remember me.

Scene 21

Anna and the Munich Virgin rise. Carl gets into the bed with his stuffed rabbit. Anna gets ready to leave.

THE THIRD MAN.   Conjugations of the verb "verlassen." To leave, to abandon, to forsake. The present tense.

CARL.   Are you leaving me alone?

ANNA.   Yes. Just for a little while. I need to take a walk. I'm restless. It's perfectly safe.

CARL.   Okay, sweetie. Don't be too long. Bunny and I are ready for bed.

ANNA.   I won't stay out long. I'll be right back.

THE THIRD MAN.   The future tense of the verb "verlassen."

CARL.   Will you be leaving me alone again tonight? I'm ready for bed.

ANNA.   I will be leaving you alone. Just for a little while.

CARL.   Who will it be tonight? The bellhop? The deskclerk? Or the maitre d'?

ANNA.   Don't be mean. You said you didn't make judgements.

CARL.   I don't. I just want to spend time with you.

ANNA.   I'll be back in time for a bedtime story.

THE THIRD MAN.   The past tense of the verb "verlassen."

CARL.   Again? Again? You left me alone last night. And the night before.

ANNA.   I can't help it. I've been a good girl for the past thirty years. Now I want to make up for lost time.

CARL.   And what am I supposed to do while you're out traipsing around with every Thomas, Deiter und Heinrich?

ANNA.   Hug bunny.

THE THIRD MAN.   There are three moods of the verb "verlassen": the indicative, the imperative, and the subjunctive. Anna and Carl are never in the same mood.

CARL.   Leave me alone.

ANNA.   Carl, don't be like that.

CARL. Why? It doesn't matter what I want. You are going to leave.

ANNA. I never stay out very long.

CARL. All I can say is if this establishment charges us for room service, they've got some nerve —

ANNA. I've got to take what opportunities come along —

CARL. I wish you wouldn't go —

ANNA. Please understand. I don't have much time. I spend as much time with you as I can, but while I still have my health ... please?

Scene 22

THE THIRD MAN. As children they fought.

CARL. We never fought, really.

ANNA. Not in a physical way. He was a sickly child.

CARL. She was very willful.

ANNA. No rough-housing. But he knew all of my weak points. My secret openings. He could be ruthless.

CARL. She'd cry at the slightest thing.

ANNA. He has a very sharp tongue.

CARL. But when one of you is very, very sick, you can't fight. It's not fair. You've got to hold it in. We never fight.

ANNA. But we had a doozy in the hotel room in Berlin.

CARL. Well, my god, Anna, even though you're sick, I have the right to get angry.

ANNA. We'd been traveling too long. We were cranky. The rooms were closing in.

CARL. I'm just saying that we should spend a little more time together. I don't get to see you alone enough. You're always restless.

ANNA. Fine. You go out without me for a change.

CARL. I'm going out for a walk.

ANNA. *(Starting to weep.)* I don't care.

CARL. When she was little, this would be the time I'd bribe her. With a comic book or an ice cream. I always had pennies saved up for these little contingencies.

ANNA. But sometimes, for the sake of my pride, I would be inconsolable. I would rush off and then feel just awful alone. Why didn't I take the bribe? *(To Carl.)* I'm going out.
CARL. To fuck?
ANNA. No, dear. The passive voice is used to emphasize the subject, to indicate the truth of the generalization. I'm going out. To get fucked.

Scene 23

Music: Kurt Weill. Anna goes over to a small cabaret table. There is a telephone on the table. The Radical Student Activist sits at another identical table, smoking, watching her.

ANNA. I'm going to enjoy Berlin without him. I'll show him. I'm going to be carefree, totally without scruples. I'll pretend I've never taught first-graders. *(Beat.)* I'm going to have a perfectly miserable time. *(The Radical Student Activist picks up the telephone. The telephone at Anna's table rings.)* Oh my goodness. My miserable time is calling me. *(Anna picks up the phone.)* Yes?
RADICAL STUDENT ACTIVIST. Are you alone, Fraülein?
ANNA. Well, uh, actually — yes, I am.
RADICAL STUDENT ACTIVIST. Gut. Du willst mal richtig durchgefickt werden, ja?
ANNA. I'm sorry. I don't speak a word of German. *(The Radical Student Activist laughs.)*
RADICAL STUDENT ACTIVIST. Ja. Even better. I said, would you like to get fucked?
ANNA. Do you always come on to single women like that?
RADICAL STUDENT ACTIVIST. Would you like it better if I bought you tall drinks with umbrellas? Told to you the stories of how hard a time my parents had during the war? Tell you how exciting I find foreign women, how they are the real women, not like the pale northern mädchen here at home? How absolutely bourgeois.
ANNA. I see. Why do you come here?

RADICAL STUDENT ACTIVIST. I don't come here for the overpriced drinks. I come here because of the bored western women who come here, who leave their tired businessmen husbands in the hotel rooms behind.

ANNA. You're cute. In a hostile way.

RADICAL STUDENT ACTIVIST. Fucking is a revolutionary act.

ANNA. Your hovel or my hotel?

Scene 24

In the Hotel Room. Anna, awake, lies in the middle of the bed. To her left, Carl sleeps, curled up. To her right, the Radical Student Activist, curled on her breast, slumbers. Anna is awake with an insomniacal desperation.

ANNA. *(Singing softly.)* Two and two are four; four and four are eight; eight and eight are sixteen; sixteen and sixteen are thirty-two —

RADICAL STUDENT ACTIVIST. *(Groggy.)* Wo ist die Toilette? *(The Radical Student Activist rises and stumbles off.)*

ANNA. In love-making, he's all fury and heat. His North Sea pounding against your Dreamer. And when you look up and see his face, red and huffing, it's hard to imagine him ever having been a newborn, tiny, wrinkled, and seven pounds. That is, until afterwards. When he rises from sleep and he walks into the bathroom. And there he exposes his soft little derrière, and you can still see the soft baby flesh. *(As the Radical Student Activist comes back into the room.)* I've got a put a name to that behind. What's your name? Wie heissen Sie?

RADICAL STUDENT ACTIVIST. *(The Radical Student Activist starts dressing in a hurry.)* Auf Wiedersehn. Next thing you'll ask for my telephone number.

ANNA. No, I won't. I was just curious —

RADICAL STUDENT ACTIVIST. Ja, ja ... und then my sign of the zodiac. I'll get cards from Hallmark und little scribblings like "I'll never forget the night we shared."

ANNA.   Forget it.

RADICAL STUDENT ACTIVIST.   There is something radical in two complete strangers committing biological necessity without having to give into bourgeois conventions of love, without breeding to produce workers for a capitalist system, without the benediction of the church, the family, the bosses —

ANNA.   I have something to confess to you. I lied to you.

RADICAL STUDENT ACTIVIST.   About what?

ANNA.   I'm not here on business. I don't specialize in corporate takeovers. I don't work on Wall Street. I only told you that because I thought that was what you wanted to hear.

RADICAL STUDENT ACTIVIST.   Okay. So you do estate planning? Income tax?

ANNA.   No. You just committed a revolutionary act with a first-grade schoolteacher who lives in low-income housing. And I'm tired. I think you should go.

RADICAL STUDENT ACTIVIST.   And your husband?

ANNA.   Not too loud. And he's not my husband. He's my brother. A maiden librarian for the San Francisco Public. *As the Radical Student Activist starts to leave.)* And by the way — the missionary position does not a revolution make. *(The Radical Student Activist leaves. Anna, depressed, lies down. Carl rises from the bed.)*

Scene 25

CARL.   And as she lay in the bed, sleepless, it swept over her — the way her classroom smelled early in the morning, before the children came. It smelled of chalk dust —

THE THIRD MAN.   It smelled of Crayola wax, crushed purple and green —

CARL.   The cedar of hamster cage shavings —

THE THIRD MAN.   The sweet wintergreen of LePage's paste —

CARL.   The wooden smell of the thick construction paper —

THE THIRD MAN.   The spillings of sticky orange drink and sour milk —

THE THIRD MAN and CARL. *(Simultaneously.)* And the insidious smell of first-grader pee.

CARL. It smelled like heaven.

ANNA. And the first thing I did each morning was put up the weather map for today on the board under the flag. A bright, smiling sun, or Miss Cloud or Mr. Umbrella. On special days I put up Suzy Snowflake. And when I opened my desk drawer, scattered like diamonds on the bottom were red, silver and gold stars. *(Beat.)* I want to go home. Carl, I want to go home.

CARL. Soon, sweetie. Very soon.

ANNA. I've had enough. I've seen all of the world I want to see. I want to wake up in my own bed. I want to sit with you at home and we'll watch the weather. And we'll wait.

CARL. We've come so far. We have to at least go to Vienna. Do you think you can hold out long enough to meet Dr. Todesrocheln? *(Anna, miserable and homesick, nods.)* That a girl. I promise you don't have to undertake his ... hydrotherapy unless you decide to. I have a friend in Vienna, a college chum, who might be able to get us some of blackmarket stuff. It's worth a shot.

ANNA. Then you'll take me home?

CARL. Then I'll take you home.

Scene 26

Music: A song such as the zither theme from The Third Man.* *Carl and Anna stand, with their luggage, in front of a door buzzer.*

CARL. First we'll just look up Harry. Then we'll cab over to Dr. Todesrocheln. *(Carl rings the buzzer. They wait. Carl rings the buzzer again. They wait. An aging Concierge comes out.)*

* See Special Note on copyright page.

Entschuldigung. Wir suchen Harry Lime? Do you speak English?

CONCIERGE. Nein. Ich spreche kein Englisch. *(Carl and the Concierge start to shout as if the other one was deaf.)*

CARL. Herr Lime? Do you know him? Herr Harry Lime?

CONCIERGE. Ach. Ach. Ja, Herr Harry Lime. You come ... too spät.

CARL. He's gone? Too spät?

CONCIERGE. Fünf minuten too spät. Er ist tot —

CARL. What?

CONCIERGE. Ja. Ein auto mit Harry splatz-machen auf der Strasse. Splatz!

ANNA. Splatz!?

CARL. Splatz?! *(It dawns on Carl and Anna what the Concierge is saying.)*

CONCIERGE. Ja, ja. Er geht über die strasse, und ein auto ... sppplllaattz!

ANNA. Oh, my god.

CONCIERGE. *(Gesturing with hands.)* Ja. Er hat auch eine rabbit. Herr Rabbit auch — sppllaattz! They are ... diggen ein grab in den Boden. Jetz.

CARL. Now? You saw this happen?

CONCIERGE. Ja. I ... saw it mit meinen own Augen. Splatz. *(As he exits.)* "Splatzen, splatzen, über alles ... "

CARL. Listen, darling. I want you to take a cab to the doctor's office.

ANNA. Where are you going?

CARL. Ich verlasse. I'll find out what happened to Harry.

ANNA. I wish you wouldn't leave....

CARL. I'll come back. Okay?

Scene 27

Anna climbs onto a table and gathers a white paper sheet around her. She huddles.

ANNA.   Some things are the same in every country. You're scared when you see the doctor, here in Vienna just like in Baltimore. And they hand you the same paper cup to fill, just like in America. Then you climb up onto the same cold metal table, and they throw a sheet around you and you feel very small. And just like at home, they tell you to wait. And you wait. *(As Anna waits, dwarfed on the table, the scene with Harry Lime and Carl unfolds. Music, such as* The Third Man* *theme, up.)*

Scene 28

On the Ferris Wheel in the Prater. Carl holds the stuffed rabbit closely.

CARL.   Why are we meeting here?
HARRY LIME.   Have you looked at the view from up here? It's quite inspiring. No matter how old I get, I always love the ferris wheel.
CARL.   I just came from your funeral.
HARRY LIME.   I'm touched, old man. Was it a nice funeral?
CARL.   What are you doing?
HARRY LIME.   It's best not to ask too many questions. The police were beginning to do that. It's extremely convenient, now and then in a man's career, to die. I've gone underground. So if you want to meet me, you have to come here.

* See Special Note on copyright page.

No one asks questions here.

CARL. Can you help us? *(Harry Lime at first does not answer. He looks at the view.)*

HARRY LIME. Where is your sister? She left you alone?

CARL. She's — she needs her rest. You were my closest friend in college.

HARRY LIME. I'll be straight with you. I can give you the drugs — but it won't help. It won't help at all. Your sister's better off with that quack Todesrocheln — we call him the Yellow Queen of Vienna — she might end up drinking her own piss, but it won't kill her.

CARL. But I thought you had the drugs —

HARRY LIME. Oh, I do. And they cost a pretty penny. For a price, I can give them to you. At a discount for old times. But you have to know, we make them up in my kitchen.

CARL. Jesus.

HARRY LIME. Why not? People will pay for these things. When they're desperate people will eat peach pits, or aloe, or egg protein — they'll even drink their own piss. It gives them hope.

CARL. How can you do this?

HARRY LIME. Listen, old man, if you want to be a millionaire, you go into real estate. If you want to be a billionaire, you sell hope. Nowadays the only place a fellow can make a decent career of it is in Mexico and Europe.

CARL. That's ... disgusting.

HARRY LIME. Look. I thought you weren't going to be ... sentimental about this. It's a business. You have to have the right perspective. Like from up here ... the people down on the street are just tiny little dots. And if you could charge $1,000, wouldn't you push the drugs? I could use a friend I can trust to help me.

CARL. When we were at Hopkins together, I thought you were God. You could hypnotize us into doing anything, and it would seem ... charming. Carl, old man, you'd say, "Just do it." Cutting classes, cribbing exams, shop-lifting, stupid undergraduate things — and I would do it. Without knowing the consequences. I would do it.

HARRY LIME.   Oh, you knew the consequences, old man. You knew. You chose not to think about them.

CARL.   I've grown old before my time from the consequences. I'm turning you in.

HARRY LIME.   I wouldn't do that, old man. *(Harry Lime pats a bulge on the inside of his trench coat.)* By the time you hit the ground, you'll be just a tiny little dot. *(Carl and Harry Lime look at each other, waiting.)* And I think you have something I want. The rabbit, bitte.

CARL.   No. You're not getting it. I'm taking it with me. *(Harry Lime puts his arms in position for a waltz and begins to sway, seductively.)*

HARRY LIME.   Come on, give it up. Come to my arms, my only one. Dance with me, my beloved, my sweet — *(Carl takes the stuffed rabbit and threatens to throw it out the window of the ferris wheel. A Strauss waltz plays very loudly, and Harry Lime and Carl waltz-struggle for the rabbit. Carl is pushed and Harry Lime waltzes off with the rabbit.)*

Scene 29

Meanwhile, back at Doctor Todesrocheln.

ANNA.   You begin to hope that the wait is proportionate to the medical expertise. My God. My feet are turning blue. Where am I? An HMO? *(Anna waits.)* The problem with being an adult is that you never forget why you're waiting. When I was a child, I could wait blissfully unaware for hours. I used to read signs and transpose letters, or count tiles in the floor. And in the days before I could read, I would make up stories about my hands — Mr. Left and Mr. Right. *(Beat.)* Mr. Left would provoke Mr. Right. Mr. Right would ignore it. The trouble would escalate, until my hands were battling each other to the death. *(Beat. Anna demonstrates.)* Then one of them would weep. Finally, they became friends again, and they'd dance — *(Anna's two hands dance together; she is unaware that Dr. Todesrocheln has entered and is watching her. He clears his throat. He wears a very dirty lab coat with pockets filled with paper and a stale doughnut. He wears a white fright wig and glasses. He also wears one sinister black glove. With relish, he carries a flask of a golden liquid.)* Oh, thank goodness.

DR. TODESROCHELN. Ja. So happy to meet you. Such an interesting specimen. I congratulate you. Very, very interesting.

ANNA. Thank you.

DR. TODESROCHELN. We must have many more such specimens from you — for the urinocryoscopy, the urinometer, the urinoglucosometer, the uroacidimeter, uroazotometer, and mein new acquirement in der laboratorium — ein urophosphometer.

ANNA. My goodness. *(Dr. Todesrocheln has put the flask down on a table. Quietly, his left hand reaches for it; the right hand stops the left.)*

DR. TODESROCHELN. Ja. Nowadays, we have learned to discover the uncharted mysteries of the fluids discharged through the urethra. We have been so primitive in the past. Doctors once could only analyze by taste and smell — but thanks to the advancement of medical science, there are no limits to our thirst for knowledge.

ANNA. Uh-huh. *(Dr. Todesrocheln's left hand seizes the flask. Trembling, with authority, his right hand replaces the flask on the table, and soothes the left hand into quietude.)*

DR. TODESROCHELN. So much data has been needlessly, carelessly destroyed in the past — the medical collections of Ravensbruck senselessly annihilated — and that is why as a scientist, I must be exacting in our measurements and recordings.

ANNA. What can I hope to find out from these ... specimens?

DR. TODESROCHELN. Ah, yes — the layman must have his due! Too much pure research und no application makes Jack ... macht Jack ... *(Dr. Todesrocheln loses his train of thought.)* Fraülein Anna — I may call you Fraülein Anna? — Let us look at the body as an alchemist, taking in straw and mud und schweinefleisch and processing it into liquid gold which purifies the body. You might say that the sickness of the body can only be cured by the health of the body. To your health! *(His left hand seizes the flask in a salute, and raises the flask to his lips. In time, the right hand brings the flask down. A brief struggle. It appears the flask might spill, but at last the right hand triumphs.)*

ANNA.   You know, even though I really grew up in the suburbs of Baltimore, I like to think of myself as an open-minded person —

DR. TODESROCHELN.   The ancient Greeks knew that the aromatic properties of the fluid could reveal the imbalances of the soul itself.... *(The left hand sneaks towards the flask.)*

ANNA.   I'm always very eager to try new foods, or see the latest John Waters film —

DR. TODESROCHELN.   — its use in the purification rites of the Aztecs is, of course, so well known that it need not be mentioned — *(The hand has grasped the flask and begins to inch it off the table.)*

ANNA.   And whenever I meet someone who cross-dresses, I always compliment him on his shoes or her earrings —

DR. TODESROCHELN.   It is the first golden drop that marks the infant's identity separate from the womb — *(The hand has slipped the flask beneath the table. His right hand is puzzled.)*

ANNA.   But still, it's important to know where your threshhold is ... and I think we're coming dangerously close to mine....

DR. TODESROCHELN.   Until the last precious amber releases the soul from the body — ashes to ashes, drop to drop — excuse me — *(His left hand, with the flask, swings in an arc behind his body; he swivels his body to the flask, his back turned to us. We can hear him drink in secrecy. With his back turned.)* Ahhh.... *(He orders himself. Composed, he turns around to face Anna again, and demurely sets down the flask. Its level is noticeably lower. Anna is aghast.)* I can sense your concern. I have been prattling on without regard to questions you must surely have —

ANNA.   Is that your real hair?

DR. TODESROCHELN.   Of course, I can not promise results, but first we must proceed by securing more samples —
ANNA.   I don't believe that's your real hair.
DR. TODESROCHELN.   I will need first of all twenty-four hours of your time for a urononcometry —
ANNA.   *(Increasingly scared.)* You look familiar to me —
DR. TODESROCHELN.   Although I can tell you from a first taste — er, test, that your uroammonica level is high — not unpleasantly so, but full-bodied —
ANNA.   Oh, my god ... I think I know who you are ... you're ... you're ... *(Anna rises to snatch his toupée. Dr. Todesrocheln suddenly stands, menacing. And the light changes.)*
DR. TODESROCHELN.   WO IST DEIN BRUDER? *(He takes off his wig and glasses and appears as the Doctor in the first scene, peeling off the black glove to reveal latex gloves underneath.)* You fool! You left your brother in the room alone! WO IST DEIN BRUDER? *(Music:* The Emperor Waltz *plays at a very loud volume. Anna, frightened, races from the doctor's office to the hotel room. We see Carl, lying stiff beneath a white sheet. To the tempo of the Strauss, Anna tries to wake him. He does not respond. Anna takes off the sheet and forces him into a sitting position, the stuffed rabbit clenched beneath his arm. Carl remains sitting, stiff, eyes open, wooden; he is still in his pajamas. Then he slumps. Anna raises him again. He remains upright for a beat, and begins to fall. Anna stops him, presses his body against hers, pulls his legs over the bed, tries to stand him up. Frozen, his body tilts against hers. She tries to make him cross the floor, his arms around her neck. She positions him in a chair, but his legs are locked in a perpendicular angle and will not touch the floor. She presses his legs to the floor. He mechanically springs forward. Then suddenly, like the doll in "E.T.A. Hoffman," the body of Carl becomes animated, but with a strange, automatic life of its own. Carl begins to waltz with Anna. Gradually, he winds down, and faltering, falls back to the bed. There is the sound of a loud alarm clock; the Doctor enters, and covers Carl with a sheet. Then he pulls a white curtain in front of the scene, as the stage lights become, for the first time, harsh, stark and white.)*

Scene 30

In the Hospital Lounge. The Doctor holds the stuffed rabbit and travel brochures in his hands. He awkwardly peels off his latex gloves.

DOCTOR. I'm sorry. There was nothing we could do.
ANNA. Yes. I know.
DOCTOR. I thought you might want to take this along with you. *(The Doctor hands Anna the stuffed rabbit.)*
ANNA. *(To the stuffed rabbit.)* There you are! *(Anna hugs the stuffed rabbit and sees the Doctor watching her.)* It's Jo-Jo. My brother's childhood rabbit. I brought it to the hospital as a little surprise. I thought it might make him feel better.
DOCTOR. Sometimes little things become important, when nothing else will help —
ANNA. Yes. *(They pause and stand together awkwardly.)* At least Carl went in his sleep. I guess that's a blessing.
DOCTOR. If one has to die from this particular disease, there are worse ways to go than pneumonia.
ANNA. I never would have believed what sickness can do to the body. *(Pause.)* Well, Doctor, I want to thank you for all you've done for my brother.
DOCTOR. I wish I could do more. By the way, housekeeping found these brochures in your brother's bedside table. I didn't know if they were important.
ANNA. *(Anna takes the brochures.)* Ah, yes. The brochures for Europe. I've never been abroad. We're going to go when he gets — *(Anna stops herself. With control.)* I must learn to use the past tense. We would have gone had he gotten better.
DOCTOR. Anna — may I call you Anna? — I, uh, if there's anything I can do —
ANNA. Thank you, but there's nothing you can do —
DOCTOR. I mean, I really would like it if you'd call me for coffee, or if ·you just want to talk about all this — *(The Doctor trails off. Anna looks at him. She smiles. He squirms.)*

ANNA.   You're very sweet. But no, I don't think so. Not now. I feel it's simply not safe for me right now to see anyone. Thanks again and goodbye. *(Anna starts to exit. The Doctor, wistful, watches her go. The lighting begins to change back to the dreamy atmosphere of the first scene. Softly, a Strauss waltz begins. Carl, perfectly well, waits for Anna. He is dressed in Austrian military regalia. They waltz off as the lights dim.)*

END OF PLAY

PROPERTY PLOT

Lounge couch
Hospital gurney with pad and sheet
White sheet, weighted (full size)
Slide projector
Berlitz Pocket Guide to Europe book (ANNA)
Lipstick (ANNA)
Pocket mirror (ANNA)
Pink triangle lapel button (CARL)
Pink slip (CARL)
White handkerchief (CARL)
Stethoscope (DOCTOR)
Clipboard (DOCTOR) with:
    ball-point pen
    medical form
    8 1/2 x 11 1/2 X-ray
Suitcase with black slip (ANNA)
Suitcase with pajama top (CARL)
2 identical stuffed rabbits (CARL, THE THIRD MAN)
Metallic wand (AIRPORT SECURITY GUARD)
Pointer (PUBLIC HEALTH OFFICIAL)
2 posters of a toilet seat in a red circle with a
    diagonal red slash (ANNA, CARL)
Educational pamphlets (ANNA, CARL)
Galoise cigarettes (2 per show) (THE THIRD MAN)
Zippo lighter (THE THIRD MAN)
Dessert tray with desserts (GARÇON)
2 passports (CARL)
2 Delft mugs (THE LITTLE DUTCH BOY AT AGE 50)
2 Germany cabaret-type telephones (ANNA, RADICAL
    STUDENT ACTIVIST)
Certs breath mints (HARRY LIME)
1,000 ml beaker containing apple juice, watered
    down (DR. TODESROCHELN)
7 travel brochures for Europe (DOCTOR)

COSTUME LIST

ANNA
Black slip
Black bra
Black panties
Reddish-brown flat shoes
Brown trench coat

CARL
Blue and white-stripped pajamas
Blue blazer (with pink triangle lapel button)
Bedroom slippers
Wire-rimmed glasses
Tan trench coat
Fedora
Sunglasses
Austrian military uniform
Tall black books with baggies

THE THIRD MAN
Long-sleeve white shirt with Velcro patch on left sleeve
Black pants
Black shoes
Long black socks
White briefs
Black clip-on necktie
Taupe trench coat
Tan fedora
Red beret
Blue beret
Black gloves
Sunglasses

DOCTOR
Latex surgical gloves (2-3 pairs per show)
Full-length lab coat with:
    pocket protector
    pens
    I.D. tag

HARRY LIME
Black trench coat
Black fedora

AIRPORT SECURITY GUARD
Security Guard patch with Velcro
Mirrored sunglasses

PUBLIC HEALTH OFFICIAL
Horned-rimmed glasses

GARÇON
Waiter vest (purple and black floral)
White apron

CUSTOMS OFFICIAL
Customs Official jacket with Dutch flag pin
Customs Official hat

THE LITTLE DUTCH BOY AT AGE 50
Dutch boy shirt (thin lined)
Dutch boy vest
Dutch boy pants (purple)
Wooden shoes (clogs)
Blond Buster Brown wig with cap attached

MUNICH VIRGIN
Short-sleeve white T-shirt

RADICAL STUDENT ACTIVIST
Gray short-sleeve T-shirt
Black boots
Long, black, wool German socks
Black leather jacket
Black cap with patent brim
Black-rimmed, John Lennon-type eyeglasses

CONCIERGE
Short-sleeve white shirt
Brown pants with suspenders
Cardigan sweater with pocket watch with chain
Tweed cap with wig

DR. TODESROCHELN
Stained white shirt with bow tie
Stained vest
Stained white pants
Stained lab coat
Fright wig
Dirty eyeglasses
1 sinister black leather glove (left hand)

STAGE HAND (optional)
White T-shirt
White pants
White sneakers
White socks
White short lab coat
White face mask with ties
White scrub cap
I.D. tag

SOUND EFFECTS

Telephone ring
Alarm clock
Clicking noise of airport security wand

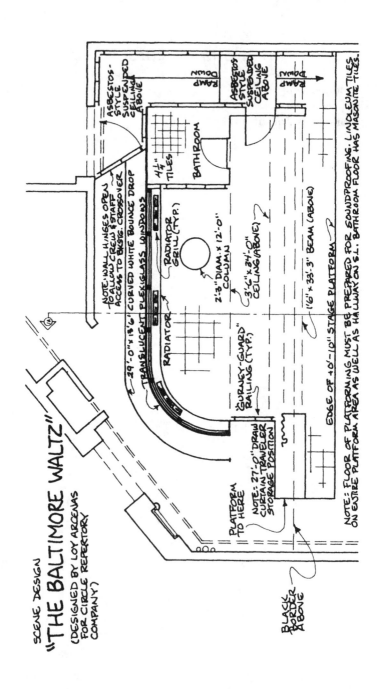

SCENE DESIGN
"THE BALTIMORE WALTZ"

(DESIGNED BY LOY ARCENAS
FOR CIRCLE REPERTORY
COMPANY)

NEW PLAYS

★ **MOTHERS AND SONS by Terrence McNally.** At turns funny and powerful, MOTHERS AND SONS portrays a woman who pays an unexpected visit to the New York apartment of her late son's partner, who is now married to another man and has a young son. Challenged to face how society has changed around her, generations collide as she revisits the past and begins to see the life her son might have led. "A resonant elegy for a ravaged generation." –NY Times. "A moving reflection on a changed America." –Chicago Tribune. [2M, 1W, 1 boy] ISBN: 978-0-8222-3183-7

★ **THE HEIR APPARENT by David Ives, adapted from Le Légataire Universel by Jean-François Regnard.** Paris, 1708. Eraste, a worthy though penniless young man, is in love with the fair Isabelle, but her forbidding mother, Madame Argante, will only let the two marry if Eraste can show he will inherit the estate of his rich but miserly Uncle Geronte. Unfortunately, old Geronte has also fallen for the fair Isabelle, and plans to marry her this very day and leave her everything in his will—separating the two young lovers forever. Eraste's wily servant Crispin jumps in, getting a couple of meddling relatives disinherited by impersonating them (one, a brash American, the other a French female country cousin)—only to have the old man kick off before his will is made! In a brilliant stroke, Crispin then impersonates the old man, dictating a will favorable to his master (and Crispin himself, of course)—only to find that rich Uncle Geronte isn't dead at all and is more than ever ready to marry Isabelle! The multiple strands of the plot are unraveled to great comic effect in the streaming rhyming couplets of French classical comedy, and everyone lives happily, and richly, ever after. [4M, 3W] ISBN: 978-0-8222-2808-0

★ **HANDLE WITH CARE by Jason Odell Williams.** Circumstances both hilarious and tragic bring together a young Israeli woman, who has little command of English, and a young American man, who has little command of romance. Is their inevitable love an accident…or is it destiny, generations in the making? "A hilarious and heartwarming romantic comedy." –NY Times. "Hilariously funny! Utterly charming, fearlessly adorable and a tiny bit magical." –Naples News. [2M, 2W] ISBN: 978-0-8222-3138-7

★ **LAST GAS by John Cariani.** Nat Paradis is a Red Sox-loving part-time dad who manages Paradis' Last Convenient Store, the last convenient place to get gas—or anything—before the Canadian border to the north and the North Maine Woods to the west. When an old flame returns to town, Nat gets a chance to rekindle a romance he gave up on years ago. But sparks fly as he's forced to choose between new love and old. "Peppered with poignant characters [and] sharp writing." –Portland Phoenix. "Very funny and surprisingly thought-provoking." –Portland Press Herald. [4M, 3W] ISBN: 978-0-8222-3232-2

DRAMATISTS PLAY SERVICE, INC.
440 Park Avenue South, New York, NY 10016 212-683-8960 Fax 212-213-1539
postmaster@dramatists.com www.dramatists.com

NEW PLAYS

★ **ACT ONE by James Lapine.** Growing up in an impoverished Bronx family and forced to drop out of school at age thirteen, Moss Hart dreamed of joining the glamorous world of the theater. Hart's famous memoir *Act One* plots his unlikely collaboration with the legendary playwright George S. Kaufman and his arrival on Broadway. Tony Award-winning writer and director James Lapine has adapted Act One for the stage, creating a funny, heartbreaking and suspenseful celebration of a playwright and his work. "…brims contagiously with the ineffable, irrational and irrefutable passion for that endangered religion called the Theater." –NY Times. "…wrought with abundant skill and empathy." –Time Out. [8M, 4W] ISBN: 978-0-8222-3217-9

★ **THE VEIL by Conor McPherson.** May 1822, rural Ireland. The defrocked Reverend Berkeley arrives at the crumbling former glory of Mount Prospect House to accompany a young woman to England. Seventeen-year-old Hannah is to be married off to a marquis in order to resolve the debts of her mother's estate. However, compelled by the strange voices that haunt his beautiful young charge and a fascination with the psychic current that pervades the house, Berkeley proposes a séance, the consequences of which are catastrophic. "…an effective mixture of dark comedy and suspense." –Telegraph (London). "A cracking fireside tale of haunting and decay." –Times (London). [3M, 5W] ISBN: 978-0-8222-3313-8

★ **AN OCTOROON by Branden Jacobs-Jenkins. Winner of the 2014 OBIE Award for Best New American Play.** Judge Peyton is dead and his plantation Terrebonne is in financial ruins. Peyton's handsome nephew George arrives as heir apparent and quickly falls in love with Zoe, a beautiful octoroon. But the evil overseer M'Closky has other plans—for both Terrebonne and Zoe. In 1859, a famous Irishman wrote this play about slavery in America. Now an American tries to write his own. "AN OCTOROON invites us to laugh loudly and easily at how naïve the old stereotypes now seem, until nothing seems funny at all." –NY Times [10M, 5W] ISBN: 978-0-8222-3226-1

★ **IVANOV translated and adapted by Curt Columbus.** In this fascinating early work by Anton Chekhov, we see the union of humor and pathos that would become his trademark. A restless man, Nicholai Ivanov struggles to dig himself out of debt and out of provincial boredom. When the local doctor, Lvov, informs Ivanov that his wife Anna is dying and accuses him of worsening her condition with his foul moods, Ivanov is sent into a downward spiral of depression and ennui. He soon finds himself drawn to a beautiful young woman, Sasha, full of hope and energy. Finding himself stuck between a romantic young mistress and his ailing wife, Ivanov falls deeper into crisis, heading toward inevitable tragedy. [8M, 8W] ISBN: 978-0-8222-3155-4

DRAMATISTS PLAY SERVICE, INC.
440 Park Avenue South, New York, NY 10016 212-683-8960 Fax 212-213-1539
postmaster@dramatists.com www.dramatists.com

NEW PLAYS

★ **I'LL EAT YOU LAST: A CHAT WITH SUE MENGERS by John Logan.** For more than 20 years, Sue Mengers' clients were the biggest names in show business: Barbra Streisand, Faye Dunaway, Burt Reynolds, Ali MacGraw, Gene Hackman, Cher, Candice Bergen, Ryan O'Neal, Nick Nolte, Mike Nichols, Gore Vidal, Bob Fosse…If her clients were the talk of the town, she was the town, and her dinner parties were the envy of Hollywood. Now, you're invited into her glamorous Beverly Hills home for an evening of dish, dirty secrets and all the inside showbiz details only Sue can tell you. "A delectable soufflé of a solo show…thanks to the buoyant, witty writing of Mr. Logan" –NY Times. "80 irresistible minutes of primo tinseltown dish from a certified master chef." –Hollywood Reporter. [1W] ISBN: 978-0-8222-3079-3

★ **PUNK ROCK by Simon Stephens.** In a private school outside of Manchester, England, a group of highly-articulate seventeen-year-olds flirt and posture their way through the day while preparing for their A-Level mock exams. With hormones raging and minimal adult supervision, the students must prepare for their future — and survive the savagery of high school. Inspired by playwright Simon Stephens' own experiences as a teacher, PUNK ROCK is an honest and unnerving chronicle of contemporary adolescence. "[A] tender, ferocious and frightning play." –NY Times. "[A] muscular little play that starts out funny and ferocious then reveals its compassion by degrees." –Hollywood Reporter. [5M, 3W] ISBN: 978-0-8222-3288-9

★ **THE COUNTRY HOUSE by Donald Margulies.** A brood of famous and longing-to-be-famous creative artists have gathered at their summer home during the Williamstown Theatre Festival. When the weekend takes an unexpected turn, everyone is forced to improvise, inciting a series of simmering jealousies, romantic outbursts, and passionate soul-searching. Both witty and compelling, THE COUNTRY HOUSE provides a piercing look at a family of performers coming to terms with the roles they play in each other's lives. "A valentine to the artists of the stage." –NY Times. "Remarkably candid and funny." –Variety. [3M, 3W] ISBN: 978-0-8222-3274-2

★ **OUR LADY OF KIBEHO by Katori Hall.** Based on real events, OUR LADY OF KIBEHO is an exploration of faith, doubt, and the power and consequences of both. In 1981, a village girl in Rwanda claims to see the Virgin Mary. Ostracized by her schoolmates and labeled disturbed, everyone refuses to believe, until impossible happenings appear again and again. Skepticism gives way to fear, and then to belief, causing upheaval in the school community and beyond. "Transfixing." –NY Times. "Hall's passionate play renews belief in what theater can do." –Time Out [7M, 8W, 1 boy] ISBN: 978-0-8222-3301-5

DRAMATISTS PLAY SERVICE, INC.
440 Park Avenue South, New York, NY 10016 212-683-8960 Fax 212-213-1539
postmaster@dramatists.com www.dramatists.com

NEW PLAYS

★ **AGES OF THE MOON by Sam Shepard.** Byron and Ames are old friends, reunited by mutual desperation. Over bourbon on ice, they sit, reflect and bicker until fifty years of love, friendship and rivalry are put to the test at the barrel of a gun. "A poignant and honest continuation of themes that have always been present in the work of one of this country's most important dramatists, here reconsidered in the light and shadow of time passed." –NY Times. "Finely wrought…as enjoyable and enlightening as a night spent stargazing." –Talkin' Broadway. [2M] ISBN: 978-0-8222-2462-4

★ **ALL THE WAY by Robert Schenkkan. Winner of the 2014 Tony Award for Best Play.** November, 1963. An assassin's bullet catapults Lyndon Baines Johnson into the presidency. A Shakespearean figure of towering ambition and appetite, this charismatic, conflicted Texan hurls himself into the passage of the Civil Rights Act—a tinderbox issue emblematic of a divided America—even as he campaigns for re-election in his own right, and the recognition he so desperately wants. In Pulitzer Prize and Tony Award–winning Robert Schenkkan's vivid dramatization of LBJ's first year in office, means versus ends plays out on the precipice of modern America. ALL THE WAY is a searing, enthralling exploration of the morality of power. It's not personal, it's just politics. "…action-packed, thoroughly gripping… jaw-dropping political drama." –Variety. "A theatrical coup…nonstop action. The suspense of a first-class thriller." –NY1. [17M, 3W] ISBN: 978-0-8222-3181-3

★ **CHOIR BOY by Tarell Alvin McCraney.** The Charles R. Drew Prep School for Boys is dedicated to the creation of strong, ethical black men. Pharus wants nothing more than to take his rightful place as leader of the school's legendary gospel choir. Can he find his way inside the hallowed halls of this institution if he sings in his own key? "[An] affecting and honest portrait…of a gay youth tentatively beginning to find the courage to let the truth about himself become known." –NY Times. "In his stirring and stylishly told drama, Tarell Alvin McCraney cannily explores race and sexuality and the graces and gravity of history." –NY Daily News. [7M] ISBN: 978-0-8222-3116-5

★ **THE ELECTRIC BABY by Stefanie Zadravec.** When Helen causes a car accident that kills a young man, a group of fractured souls cross paths and connect around a mysterious dying baby who glows like the moon. Folk tales and folklore weave throughout this magical story of sad endings, strange beginnings and the unlikely people that get you from one place to the next. "The imperceptible magic that pervades human existence and the power of myth to assuage sorrow are invoked by the playwright as she entwines the lives of strangers in THE ELECTRIC BABY, a touching drama." –NY Times. "As dazzling as the dialogue is dreamful." –Pittsburgh City Paper. [3M, 3W] ISBN: 978-0-8222-3011-3

DRAMATISTS PLAY SERVICE, INC.
440 Park Avenue South, New York, NY 10016 212-683-8960 Fax 212-213-1539
postmaster@dramatists.com www.dramatists.com